OVERCOMING ADVERSITY:
SHARING THE AMERICAN DREAM

CESAR CHAVEZ

MASON CREST PUBLISHERS
PHILADELPHIA

OVERCOMING ADVERSITY:
SHARING THE AMERICAN DREAM

Charles Barkley

Halle Berry

Cesar Chavez

Kenny Chesney

George Clooney

Johnny Depp

Tony Dungy

Jermaine Dupri

Jennifer Garner

Kevin Garnett

John B. Herrington

Salma Hayek

Vanessa Hudgens

Samuel L. Jackson

Norah Jones

Martin Lawrence

Bruce Lee

Eva Longoria

Malcolm X

Carlos Mencia

Chuck Norris

Barack Obama

Rosa Parks

Bill Richardson

Russell Simmons

Carrie Underwood

Modern American
 Indian Leaders

OVERCOMING ADVERSITY:
SHARING THE AMERICAN DREAM

CESAR CHAVEZ

BRIAN BAUGHAN

MASON CREST PUBLISHERS
PHILADELPHIA

ABOUT CROSS-CURRENTS

When you see this logo, turn to the Cross-Currents section at the back of the book. The Cross-Currents features explore connections between people, places, events, and ideas.

Produced by OTTN Publishing, Stockton, New Jersey

Mason Crest Publishers
370 Reed Road
Broomall, PA 19008
www.masoncrest.com

First printing

1 3 5 7 9 8 6 4 2

Library of Congress Cataloging-in-Publication Data

Baughan, Brian.
   Cesar Chavez / Brian Baughan.
      p. cm. — (Sharing the American dream: overcoming adversity)
   Includes bibliographical references.
   ISBN 978-1-4222-0582-2 (hardcover) — ISBN 978-1-4222-0739-0 (pbk.)
   1. Chavez, Cesar, 1927-1993—Juvenile literature. 2. Labor leaders—United
States—Biography—Juvenile literature. 3. Mexican American migrant agricultural
laborers—Biography—Juvenile literature. 4. United Farm Workers—History—Juvenile
literature. 5. Migrant agricultural laborers—Labor unions—United
States—History—Juvenile literature. I. Title.
   HD6509.C48B38 2008
   331.88'13092—dc22
   [B]
                                           2008023067

OVERCOMING ADVERSITY:
SHARING THE AMERICAN DREAM

TABLE OF CONTENTS

CHAPTER ONE

ANOTHER VICTORY

The long line of cars emerged from the thick morning fog. It was a heartening sight for lawyer Jerry Cohen. He counted roughly 500 vehicles, which meant the caravan could be carrying as many as 3,000 farmworkers. And Cohen knew each of them was there to show support for his client and their dedicated leader, Cesar Chavez.

On that day, February 27, 1968, Cesar was scheduled to appear before the Kern County Superior Court for defying an injunction filed on behalf of Giumarra Vineyards Corporation, California's largest grower of table grapes. Giumarra, located in the southern California town of Delano, had won the injunction to restrict the number of union members picketing on its fields. Cesar, acting on behalf of his union, the United Farm Workers Organizing Committee (UFWOC), believed he had to break the law. UFWOC was in the middle of a strike, and if it was going to win a fair employment contract from the grape growers, those picket lines *had* to be full of people.

The growers feared the large movement Cesar Chavez had organized. They hoped he would receive the heaviest possible sentence—a two-month jail term and a total of $12,000 in fines. And yet, as he passed reporters on his way to the Bakersfield

Cesar Chavez speaks with workers in a California vineyard, 1968. A tireless advocate for the rights of agricultural laborers, Cesar was the driving force behind the farmworkers movement.

courthouse, Cesar hardly fit the image of someone on his way to jail. Visibly frail after going 12 days on a spiritual fast, this small, quiet man walked up the courthouse steps with the assistance of two other men.

Nor did the 3,000 farmworkers at the courthouse look menacing or conduct themselves like lawbreakers. The opposite was true. Kneeling in prayer in front of the courthouse, or standing along its walls inside, the men and women remained silent or sang quietly—a humble expression of their solidarity with Cesar. They were carrying out the kind of peaceful protest their leader always expected from them. In fact, he had begun his most recent fast as a way to illustrate the importance of nonviolence. He wanted to recommit UFWOC to its nonviolent strategy, and he refused to eat while there was any chance of a violent outbreak. "No union movement is worth the death of one farmworker or his child or one grower and his child," he had declared shortly after beginning the fast.

The Kern County Superior Court judge, faced with the compelling witness of hundreds of farmworkers, decided against imprisoning Cesar that day and postponed the hearing until April. Several months later, Giumarra dropped its legal complaint against Cesar and the union, to avoid the accompanying bad publicity. It was a small but meaningful victory, one of many within the larger movement that Cesar and the farmworkers called *La Causa,* "the Cause."

Although Giumarra had given in on this particular injunction issue, it and the other grape-growing companies continued to deny the farmworkers' demands for fair hiring practices, decent wages, and safe working conditions. And so the strike, which had begun in 1965, would continue for two more years, until 1970. Cesar's 1968 fast, which lasted 25 days, took a heavy toll: he lost 30 pounds. And there were more fasts to come.

Cesar Chavez—along with UFWOC lawyer Jerry Cohen (left) and Joseph F. Donnelly, chairman of the Catholic Bishops' Committee on Farm Labor—examines a union contract, 1970. Seated at right, and prepared to sign the agreement on behalf of Giumarra Vineyards Corporation, is John Giumarra Jr.

There were also more rallies, marches, strikes, court hearings, and boycotts. But with each campaign Cesar led, more supporters emerged. Members of Congress, union leaders, religious figures, celebrities, students, and millions of everyday people would all play a part in the farmworker movement that Cesar and a few other associates began in the early 1960s.

The welfare of the farmworkers was always a central concern for Cesar. He knew the struggles of agricultural laborers because he had been one himself. When he was a child, he and his family had searched for a living wage during the Great Depression— the economic disaster that began in 1929 and lasted more than a decade—and Cesar's search continued into adulthood. In his native Arizona and in California, he experienced the exploitation that thousands of other Chicanos faced in the fields, as well as the discrimination they suffered elsewhere. He dreamed of a movement that would spell the end of injustice against his people.

A Simple Desire

One of the country's most celebrated Chicano leaders, Cesar cofounded the National Farm Workers Association, which later became the United Farm Workers (UFW). He was president from the union's start in 1962 until his death in 1993. Some of the union's most famous campaigns, such as the 1965–1970 grape strike and its accompanying boycott, attracted millions of supporters and ushered the concerns of the country's farmworkers into the international spotlight.

Like all great labor leaders, Cesar had a natural gift for strategizing and organizing people around a common mission. He inspired his union to take a firm stance against the powerful, the wealthy, and the politically connected. Rather than targeting just a few large companies, however, Cesar and the UFW pursued an overarching agenda: to expose the ways in which the U.S. farm system oppressed its workers, and to change that system. With the right vision and strategy, Cesar believed, reform was possible.

Cesar was a devout Catholic whose life centered on sacrifice, compassion, and nonviolence. He insisted that his union hold these spiritual values sacred, which earned him comparisons to other leaders who drew inspiration from their religious convictions, including Dr. Martin Luther King Jr. (1929–1968) and Mohandas Gandhi (1869–1948), the leader of the movement for Indian independence and a personal hero to Cesar.

READ MORE

Want to know more about Dr. Martin Luther King Jr. and other major influences on Cesar Chavez? Turn to page 46.

Cesar in his office at UFW headquarters in Delano, California. Behind him are photos of two of his inspirations: Senator Robert F. Kennedy and Mohandas K. Gandhi.

Robert F. Kennedy, a prominent U.S. senator and ally of many civil rights leaders, called his friend Cesar Chavez "one of the heroic figures of our time." Many Americans would agree, and yet for a hero, his mission was humble: he simply didn't want farmworkers to suffer the hardships he knew as a child. In an interview with a reporter following the activist's funeral in 1993, Cesar's son Paul said:

> He talked about going to the eighth grade and having to stop going to school to help put food on the table. He said, "I don't ever want to have another parent have to make the decisions that my parents made. That's why I'm doing this, and why I'm going to keep on doing this. Very basic."

CHAPTER TWO

CROOKED LINES

As the family's oldest son, Cesar Chavez was expected to be a skilled farmer like his father, Librado. Cesar enthusiastically accepted the role. When he was a young boy, he shadowed Librado all over their 80-acre farm in Yuma County, Arizona, peppering him with questions as they harnessed their horses, dug irrigation ditches, and plowed the fields. He relentlessly tackled the chores and kept tabs on the tasks he excelled at the most. He was most proud of his cutting skills, and he considered himself the best watermelon cutter in the family.

This snapshot of Cesar's childhood depicts an immigrant family that has attained the American Dream. In a way, the picture is accurate, at least in the beginning. Cesar's grandfather, Cesario, had overcome great poverty in Mexico to settle a large tract of land in Arizona's North Gila Valley, which he passed on to Librado. The Chavezes had made a decent living, with Librado and his wife, Juana, taking in steady income through additional assets that included a grocery store, a garage, and a pool hall.

Cesar Estrada Chavez was born on March 31, 1927, two years before the stock market crash that marked the beginning of the Great Depression. At first, the Chavezes skirted the financial ruin

Lettuce fields in Arizona's Gila Valley. Cesar Chavez spent the first 10 years of his life on his family's 80-acre farm in the valley.

that other families had suffered. The family was even secure enough to extend credit to debt-ridden customers at its grocery store. Yet the national economy's steady decline, coupled with the region's first drought in 66 years, would eventually spell the end of the Chavez homestead.

Equal Shares

Whatever the financial situation, young Cesar always could take refuge in the comforts of his tight-knit community. There was the Chavez backyard with its big fire hole, where dozens of relatives would gather to roast corn and tell each other stories. There were also the nearby homes of his aunts and uncles, which would regularly open up to the Chavez children.

There was also the remarkable closeness between Cesar and his siblings. Rita, the oldest of the children, and Cesar, the second oldest, were inseparable. They fondly called each other *tita* and *tito* (short for "little sister" and "little brother"). Cesar also got along well with his brother Richard, who was two years younger. Both Rita and Richard often deferred to Cesar's judgment. He had a knack for delegating farming duties to make sure all the chores were done.

Juana did her part to ensure that all her children—she and Librado eventually had three girls and three boys—got along. She insisted that the children understand and practice generosity, and there were penalties for disobeying her. "She would try to give us equal shares," Cesar recalled to Jacques Levy, author of *Cesar Chavez: Autobiography of La Causa*, "but if one of us complained, 'I got the smaller piece,' she would take them away from everybody." She even encouraged her children to be charitable with strangers, sending them out to the streets to look for *trampitas* (little tramps) in need of a warm dinner.

Cesar unfortunately did not feel that harmony at school, where he believed his teachers never gave him the respect he deserved. During that era, many Chicanos lived as second-class citizens. Although Cesar and many of his schoolmates spoke Spanish at home, they were forbidden to speak that language in front of their teachers. Doing so would earn them a harsh scolding or a punishment such as paddling. Cesar, who was a shy boy, considered the embarrassment of any rebuke worse than the pain of any paddling. Fortunately, the schoolhouse was not the only place where Cesar learned. At home, Juana loved reciting *dichos* (sayings or proverbs) to the children, while Cesar's grandmother oversaw their formal Catholic education.

California

Hard times hit the family eventually. Librado and Juana first had to sell all their businesses. Then, as their debts escalated, the bank threatened to reclaim the Chavez homestead. When Cesar was 10, Librado left the family to look for work in California. This would be no easy task, as by that point there were nearly 300,000 migrant workers vying for jobs on the state's farms.

But Librado did find a job, and soon Juana and the kids left Arizona to join him. They piled into the old family car and headed for Oxnard, a city located in an agricultural region 55 miles north of Los Angeles. The Chavezes had hoped this foray into California would be temporary and that they would earn enough money to pay their debts and resume the life they had known in Yuma. However, they were in for a rude awakening. In Oxnard and throughout California, there was a great surplus of workers, meaning that farmers could pay dismally low wages while tens of thousands of workers would compete to fill the available jobs. The Chavezes were often homeless; many times they slept under a piece of canvas strung to a tree. At one point, they had to eat wild mustard greens to avoid going hungry.

In addition to these hardships, Cesar was deeply troubled by the desperate competition he saw among neighbors. It was saddening, for instance, to see the field hands fight each other over the few empty harvest baskets that the growers provided for them. He missed that sense of community that had made life in Arizona so memorable.

In February 1939, the family learned that their Yuma homestead was up for public auction, and they returned to Arizona.

All of Librado's attempts to reclaim the land had failed. The new owners had no intention of preserving the farm. With the Chavez family standing by, the tractors rolled in to destroy the trees and fill in the irrigation canals. The sight of the unforgiving tractors tearing up the land was devastating. Looking back on the scene years later, Cesar wondered why he was denied the plantation life that was part of the original Chavez plan. "If we had stayed there," he told Jacques Levy, "possibly I would have been a grower. God writes in exceedingly crooked lines."

Formative Experiences

With no other options, Cesar and his family returned to California. They eked out a hand-to-mouth existence as migrant

Migrant workers toil in a field. From the days of Cesar Chavez's youth to the present, migrant laborers have done much of the backbreaking work that puts food on American tables.

workers. Librado Chavez toiled from sunup till sundown in the fields. Juana and the children joined him after school and on weekends. The work was backbreaking, paid very little, and required the family to move continually. When a planting or harvest on one farm had been completed, they went on to another farm. When one crop's picking season was over, they had to look for work picking another crop.

On some farms, the Chavezes stayed in one of the crude dwellings for migrant workers, which had no electricity and no indoor plumbing. Sometimes, however, no housing was available and the family had to sleep outdoors. Though living conditions were terrible, the Chavezes avoided government-run labor camps, which at least had better sanitation, because these camps were too cramped to offer the family any semblance of dignity.

In 1942, after a car accident left Librado Chavez seriously injured, Cesar dropped out of school and went to work full time in the fields. He had only completed the eighth grade, but he believed he needed to make more money to support the family. Although Cesar would have a lifelong passion for education, he did not totally regret the decision to drop out. He had attended dozens of schools in California, many for only a few days or weeks, which made learning very difficult. And, as a Chicano, he suffered a variety of slights, including racist comments by classmates and punishment from teachers for speaking Spanish.

READ MORE

The Grapes of Wrath described life in California's labor camps during the Great Depression. For a profile of the author, see page 48.

There was at least one bright moment during his teenage years: in 1943 he met his future wife, Helen Fabela. She was working in a malt shop in Delano, a town not far from

McFarland, where the Chavezes were living. Helen was 15 years old, and she made an immediate impression on Cesar. The two shared an important connection, as she, too, came from a family of migrant workers.

They began dating, but were soon separated when Cesar enlisted in the U.S. Navy. Although he never saw combat, Cesar considered his time in the navy full of awful experiences. Along with the regimentation of military life, he hated the discrimination that nonwhite servicemen faced. It was during a weekend leave in Delano that his anger about segregation boiled over into action. Indignant over the requirement that he sit in the "colored" section of a movie theater, Cesar sat in the whites-only section instead, a violation for which he spent an hour in jail.

READ MORE

To learn more about segregation in the United States—and the legal cases that helped end it—see page 49.

Get Out If You Can

Later, Cesar was honorably discharged from the navy, and within a year he married Helen. They had their first child, Fernando, the following year, and after a short time in northern California, they settled in a barrio of San Jose called Sal Si Puedes (meaning "Get Out If You Can"). The neighborhood's name bluntly described its economic situation, and by that point, Cesar and Helen Chavez had to scramble to support two more children, Sylvia and Linda.

Shortly after settling in Sal Si Puedes, Cesar befriended two men who would profoundly influence his life. The first was Father Donald McDonnell, a socially conscious Catholic priest committed to helping seasonal Mexican workers known as braceros and visiting prisoners in the city jail. Cesar volunteered to help the priest with offering Mass to the inmates.

During their times working alongside each other, Cesar would ask McDonnell to recommend books that might develop his faith or his ideas about social justice. By that point, Cesar had familiarized himself with labor issues by reading the newspapers. He welcomed the new insights he gained through his reading of works by the union leader and socialist Eugene Debs as well as the writings of spiritual thinkers. A biography of Gandhi, along with Gandhi's own writings, had the strongest effect on Cesar. He was fascinated by the Indian independence movement and the nonviolent tactics its leader used against the British colonial authorities.

Cesar's second mentor was Fred Ross, whom he met in 1952. Ross was founder of the Community Service Organization (CSO), which sought to increase the political influence of Chicanos through voter registration and citizenship classes. He was eager to find more partners, and through the recommendation of McDonnell, Ross approached Cesar as a CSO prospect.

Before long, Cesar was working tirelessly as a "bird dog," a volunteer canvasser going door to door to register voters and recruit new organization members. The first registration drive lasted 85 days—and Cesar worked all but one of them. He took off that single day only because Ross had urged him to spend some time with his family.

The Next Project

As the CSO's star apprentice, Cesar helped establish a new chapter in San Jose. Soon CSO leaders were convinced to hire him as a full-time organizer so that he could continue to found chapters. He was assigned to his old neighborhood of Oxnard. There, Cesar decided to expand his mission beyond finding more CSO members. At the time, farmworkers were involved in a controversy involving local growers and the Farm Placement

Fred Ross, founder of the Community Service Organization, was one of Cesar Chavez's early mentors. Here, Ross marches with Cesar at a 1982 demonstration.

Service, a government agency charged with directing agricultural laborers to the places where they were needed at a given time. By law, local workers were entitled to the jobs available through the Farm Placement Service. But the agency was conspiring with local growers to fill the jobs with braceros, who would work for less.

The campaign Cesar Chavez led thoroughly documented the process that favored the braceros and shed light on the system's shady dealings. For a limited period, at least, the Farm Placement Service had no choice but to fulfill its obligation to the local workers.

Cesar's success in Oxnard earned him a promotion to CSO executive director in 1959. He had proven that he was an effective leader whose organizing talents could achieve real results. More important, he learned that the most pressing concern for farmworkers was not voter registration or U.S. citizenship, but receiving fair treatment from their employers. This conclusion led to his idea for the next project: the creation of a farmworkers union. Cesar's plan attracted the full support of many CSO members, including Fred Ross and Dolores Huerta, another Ross protégé and accomplished organizer who had begun working for the CSO in 1955.

READ MORE

To learn more about the Bracero Program, turn to page 50.

To establish the farmworkers union, Cesar needed to get a vote of approval from CSO's general members. The vote was scheduled for the organization's annual convention in Calexico, California, on March 31, 1962. There, to the anguish of many CSO leaders, the members voted down the union proposal. Cesar's calm reaction surprised everyone in the hall. He stood to address the convention. "I have an announcement to make," he said. "I resign." It was Cesar's 35th birthday.

The CSO's members were devastated. No one wanted Cesar to leave, but his mind was set. He was determined to organize the farmworkers, with or without the CSO.

CHAPTER THREE

VIVA LA CAUSA!

Cesar Chavez and the other leaders eagerly awaited the first convention of the National Farm Workers Association (NFWA), scheduled for September 30, 1962, in Fresno, California. Since leaving the CSO, Cesar had been scrambling to build up the NFWA, which he and a few close associates had launched. At the convention, they hoped to make a good impression on the fledgling union's members. The workers, after all, had taken a chance on the NFWA only because it promised to stand up for their rights. This meeting would reveal whether Cesar and the other NFWA leaders could make good on their word.

Cesar had asked his cousin, Manuel Chavez, to arrive in Fresno a few days early to locate a hall for the event. It was not an easy assignment, as the NFWA budget had no money to rent the space. Manuel acted fast and summoned his natural charm as a car salesman to secure the reservation, promising that he and his associates would "pass the hat" later to pay the rental fee.

Such was the nature of the six-month drive Cesar had led to establish the NFWA from its headquarters in Delano. By necessity the drive had been largely a family effort, done on the fly and with the scarcest of resources. But Cesar also received vital assistance from two key people he had recruited to help lead the NFWA: Dolores Huerta, who cofounded the association and became its vice president, and Gil Padilla, another CSO veteran.

Even Cesar did not know how challenging it would be to organize a new support base without CSO's personnel and financial support. "What I didn't know was that we would go through hell because it was all but an impossible task," he later remembered. There was hardly any time to be daunted as he crisscrossed the surrounding counties by foot and by car to reach new recruits. Unable to afford a babysitter, he often brought his children—by this time, Cesar and Helen had eight kids—and his brother Richard's children along to help distribute thousands of leaflets to people on the streets. By the end of those short six months, Cesar had covered thousands of miles and spoken with tens of thousands of workers.

The First Campaign

At the NFWA convention in September, Cesar and the other leaders present-ed—and won approval from the general members for—a variety of proposals. Members accepted the union's primary objectives of winning for workers a minimum wage of $1.50

Cesar consults with Dolores Huerta, 1968. A gifted organizer and tough negotiator, Huerta cofounded the National Farm Workers Association and hammered out union contracts with growers.

per hour and unemployment insurance (payment to cover workers' basic needs in the event they lost their jobs). They also voted to adopt an NFWA flag, which included a stylized eagle (a symbol of the mighty Aztec civilization of Mexico); a motto, *Viva La Causa!* ("Long live the cause!"); and a *corrido* (ballad) that served as the union's official anthem.

By 1965, the NFWA had 1,200 members and a core group of leaders. It had also formed a partnership with the Agricultural Workers Organizing Committee (AWOC), a California-based group composed mostly of Filipino workers. AWOC, which represented many grape pickers in Delano and beyond, had approached the NFWA with an opportunity to participate in its first public campaign. AWOC workers, like those in the NFWA,

This poster was produced for the NFWA in support of the Delano grape strike. The poster says, "Long live Chavez," "Long live the cause," and "Long live the strike."

had grown weary of receiving substandard wages from the table-grape and wine-grape growers. To force the growers to offer fair compensation, AWOC wanted to put a halt to grape production, and it wanted the NFWA as its strike partner.

The decision now facing Cesar and the rest of the NFWA leaders was not easy. While the union had grown dramatically, many members were still not paying their dues, which meant the NFWA did not have an adequate strike fund to finance the effort. If the strike didn't succeed in winning a decent contract, the workers would have sacrificed their wages in vain.

However, the NFWA wanted to show its solidarity with AWOC. Cesar also recognized a large-scale strike as a great way of building awareness for the movement beyond Delano. The leadership settled the matter by putting the question of a *huelga* (strike) to a general vote. Cesar called an official meeting of the NFWA at a church in Delano. There, an audience of 1,500 people voted to strike, and they affirmed their enthusiasm with shouts of *"Viva la causa!" "Viva la huelga!" "Viva la unión!"*

The Movement Grows

A total of 1,200 workers participated in the strike, which began in September 1965 and affected an area of 400 square miles. As anticipated, the growers recruited other workers, called strike-breakers, to replace the workers who had walked off the job. Cesar responded by urging union members to recruit the strikebreakers to their side. Uncertain that their tactics would succeed, the growers soon resorted to intimidating protesters, using their tractors to spray dust on people along the picket lines. Some men even physically attacked picketers, including Cesar.

As the campaign continued into the winter of 1965–1966, Cesar found opportunities to broaden support for the farmworkers and take the fight to the most powerful growers in the region.

Early on, he recognized the overwhelming influence that consumers had over the policies of two companies, Schenley Industries and DiGiorgio Fruit Corporation. If customers could be convinced not to buy grapes from these companies, the economic impact would be devastating. So the NFWA declared a boycott. Cesar sent farmworkers and volunteers to New York and other major cities, where they asked consumers to refuse to buy grapes from the targeted companies.

More opportunities to raise support came through invitations for Cesar to give talks about the farmworker movement. He received a huge audience at the University of California at Berkeley, which by that time had become a hotbed for civil rights action and a source of funding for activists. He also began networking with fellow union leaders like Walter Reuther, president of the United Automobile Workers, who pledged $5,000 on behalf of the UAW to the grape strike fund.

One event in 1966 that attracted a massive amount of support was the 300-mile march from Delano to the California State Capitol Building in Sacramento. With Cesar leading, about 100 marchers set out to raise awareness for the farmworker cause on March 17, beginning what would become the country's longest protest march ever. Cesar discovered early on that his feet weren't prepared for such a long journey. Only eight miles from Delano, he noticed that a massive blister had formed on one foot. By the 25-mile point, his whole leg was swollen and several blisters had formed. With help from a cane, however, he pressed on.

An estimated 10,000 had joined the march by the time it reached the State Capitol steps in Sacramento on Easter Sunday. The great show of support was effective: even before the marchers' arrival in Sacramento, Cesar had received word from Schenley Industries that it wanted to negotiate with the NFWA.

On the road to Sacramento: NFWA supporters during the historic 300-mile march from Delano to California's State Capitol, 1966. The march, led by Cesar Chavez, generated a great deal of publicity for the farmworkers' cause.

In August the DiGiorgio Fruit Corporation finally agreed to permit workers at one of its ranches to decide whether they wanted to be represented by a union and, if so, which one. The election would be a serious test for the NFWA, as the competing union was the powerful and well-established International Brotherhood of Teamsters. DiGiorgio favored the Teamsters, which would not be negotiating in the best interests of the farmworkers because it maintained secret ties with the growers.

"Let's Go Get Another One"

To increase their strength, the NFWA and AWOC decided to merge as the United Farm Workers Organizing Committee

(UFWOC). UFWOC would be affiliated with the AFL-CIO, the largest federation of unions in the United States. It proved to be a wise move: UFWOC won the DiGiorgio election, with 530 votes to the Teamsters' 331. The victory was important, but it was only one of many needed to win the overall strike. There were other grape growers that needed to be convinced to accept unionization. Speaking at the victory celebration, Cesar kept the union focused on its mission. "I said, 'Okay, we've won,' " he later recounted to Jacques Levy, " 'but we can't sit on our laurels. Let's go get another one.' "

By the middle of 1967, with the grape strike in its second year, Cesar was looking for a way to apply additional pressure on the growers. He also wanted to continue broadening support for La Causa. UFWOC decided that the most appropriate action was another boycott against the most powerful local grower, Giumarra Vineyards Corporation. Cesar again sent farmworkers and other volunteers out to various cities, where they asked consumers to refuse to buy Giumarra grapes.

Giumarra countered by placing the labels of other growers on its grapes in an attempt to fool consumers and stores participating in the boycott. Undeterred, Cesar responded by calling on customers to boycott not just Giumarra grapes but all California table grapes. It was a tall order, but by this point, UFWOC had won the support of a wide coalition of fellow unions, faith-based groups, students, minority groups, and general consumers.

The fight thus continued—on the production front with the strike, and on the consumer front with the boycott. By early 1968, however, Cesar believed that the movement was falling off course. UFWOC officers were shirking their duties, staying holed up in the union offices rather than organizing workers in the fields. More upsetting still, pro-union picketers were resorting to violence against the growers and their supporters. Cesar even confiscated guns from a few individuals who had not responded to his call for peaceful protest.

A Different Weapon

In the middle of February, Cesar made the announcement that he had begun a water-only fast. Until union members recommitted themselves to nonviolence, the only nourishment he would take would be a communion wafer each day at Mass. To conserve his energy, he retreated to Forty Acres, UFWOC's headquarters.

There were different responses to Cesar's decision to fast. Some union members couldn't relate to his religious devotion, and a few even quit. But most people in his inner circle, as well as the vast majority of his general supporters, supported his need for penance. Visitors flocked to the makeshift camp at Forty Acres, and eventually the area became a tent city, with as many as 1,000 people joining Cesar every day to celebrate Mass.

More and more people turned their attention to La Causa, particularly after the union's dramatic display of solidarity with Cesar as he faced the court for disobeying a strike injunction. After the judge decided not to impose a penalty on him, Cesar returned to Forty Acres to continue his fast and stir up more support for the strike. Finally, after having refused food for 25 days, Cesar announced the end of his fast, signifying to everyone that the union had successfully heeded his call for nonviolence.

READ MORE

To learn more about Cesar's ideas on fasting, turn to page 51.

On March 10, some 6,000 people gathered for a special communion to mark the end of the fast. Among the attendees was Robert F. Kennedy, who had recently befriended Cesar and offered him support. Within a week, Kennedy—a U.S. senator representing New York—would announce his decision to run for president of the United States.

As Cesar took communion, he was flanked by his mother and Kennedy. Cesar had prepared an official statement, but because the fast had left him too weak to address the crowd, an assistant read the statement for him. His words described a victory that the workers could achieve despite all the obstacles in their way:

> Our struggle is not easy. Those who oppose our cause are rich and powerful, and they have many allies in high places. We are poor. Our allies are few. But we have something the rich do not own. We have our own bodies and spirits and the justice of our cause as our weapons.

Senator Robert F. Kennedy (left) was among 6,000 supporters who joined Cesar as he marked the end of his 25-day fast for nonviolence, March 10, 1968.

CHAPTER FOUR

A FEARSOME RIVAL

In 1970, a number of California grape growers finally began negotiating with the farmworkers after holding out against the boycott Cesar had first called in 1965. He celebrated the victory by eating his first bunch of grapes in five years. He paused to savor the fruit, which he called "sweet grapes of justice."

Endless picketing had put the needed pressure on the growers. So had the grape boycott, which had begun in California and expanded to include 14 million Americans. Even customers in Great Britain and other European countries had agreed to stop buying grapes. La Causa had grown so popular that Cesar made the cover of *Time* magazine. The publicity was flattering, but he was most proud that the boycott and the picketing campaigns had remained true to the ways of nonviolence.

The celebration over the strike's end was a short one, however, because

In July 1969, when *Time* magazine put Cesar on its cover, the grape strike was in its fourth year.

UFWOC immediately received news that the Teamsters had suddenly signed 30 contracts in the Salinas Valley. This region, located south of San Jose along California's central coast, employs a large segment of the state's farmworkers to pick lettuce, broccoli, strawberries, tomatoes, and several other crops. Here, in what many call "the salad bowl of the world," the Teamsters had staked their claim. Their sweetheart deals with growers had left virtually no negotiating power for the workers. Worse, many growers were ready to fire any worker who refused to accept the Teamsters as their union. Similar deals took place in the San Joaquin Valley and the Imperial Valley, located in southeastern California near the Arizona border.

"A New Age"

Cesar believed that the union had to take the fight to the Teamsters and challenge the fairness of the contracts the Teamsters had concluded with growers. If UFWOC lost its influence in the central coast, it could lose the gains it had made thus far. Cesar pushed for immediate action, and another march and rally was scheduled in late July.

At the rally in the town of Salinas that ended the four-day march, Cesar made it clear to the 3,000 supporters assembled that the union wouldn't tolerate the secret contracts that had left farmworkers out to dry. "It's tragic that these men have not yet come to understand that we are in a new age, a new era," he said. "No longer can a couple of white men sit together and write the destinies of all the Chicanos and Filipino workers in this valley."

Cesar first petitioned for UFWOC to be granted new elections at the growers' ranches, which would give workers the option to decide between UFWOC and the Teamsters as their union. As negotiations began between UFWOC and the growers,

Cesar wanted to apply pressure on the growers without resorting to a strike or a boycott, each of which would demand great sacrifices of workers. However, when the talks eventually fell apart, Cesar believed he had no choice but to mount another large-scale campaign—a strike against non-union lettuce growers.

A Grave Danger

As before, he laid out the battle on multiple fronts, with picketing, work stoppages, acts of civil disobedience, and legal suits. The strategy was the same, but this time the strikers were up against a totally different opposition. Early on, the Teamster leaders demonstrated that they had no qualms about using force. They recruited a squad of goons who set up temporary headquarters in a hotel in Salinas. These men masqueraded as defenders of the public good by assembling as "citizens committees." In reality, they were loyal only to the growers, who gave their silent approval to crush their opposition by any means necessary. Some of the Teamsters relied on their fists; others wielded baseball bats and chains.

Cesar continually pleaded for nonviolent action on the picket lines. On more than a few occasions, however, his words fell on deaf ears. Some picketers, fed up with the cruelty of the Teamster goons, began throwing rocks at their enemies' vehicles or laying nails in the road to flatten their car tires. Cesar's case for peace was perhaps never as crucial as it was during the lettuce strike. Violent protest not only threatened to lose the public's sympathy; it also could exacerbate a climate that already had put Cesar in grave danger. At the time, he was receiving bomb threats. But Cesar refused to let security concerns distract him from his mission. "The only way they could protect me is to put me in a bullet-proof tube," he told Jacques Levy, "or to put me thirty feed underground in a silo. And what work could I do then?"

Cesar faced frequent threats against his life, but he refused to let that inhibit his work. Here he marches in New York City to drum up support for the lettuce boycott. Coretta Scott King, widow of slain civil rights leader Martin Luther King Jr., is at his side. Inset: A union poster urging people to boycott lettuce and grapes.

To make matters worse, it appeared that the California courts were siding with the growers. In September 1970, a superior court judge had issued permanent injunctions against picketing 30 growers. Without the picket as a viable protest tactic, Cesar had no choice but to focus on a nationwide boycott of the world's largest lettuce grower, Bud Antle Corporation, and other non-UFWOC lettuce growers. This boycott was particularly bold, since lettuce, unlike grapes, is a staple—a basic food for which there is a constant high demand. But customers again rose up to support the farmworkers.

Cesar Goes to Jail

Despite the popular support for UFWOC, the courts didn't condone the tactics of the campaign. On December 4, 1970, a judge sentenced Cesar to jail on two counts of contempt of court, ordering that Cesar remain imprisoned until he instructed his union to call off the boycott against Bud Antle. Cesar refused to bow to the pressure, and as 2,000 union members stood in silent support at the courthouse, he was ushered to his jail cell.

UFWOC's lawyers didn't sit by while Cesar was in jail. They exercised his rights to appeal to a higher court. On Christmas Eve, 20 days after he was sentenced, the California Supreme Court ordered his release pending a review of the case. As he left the jail, Cesar was greeted by 400 union supporters. His words reassured them that nothing could break his resolve. "My spirit was never in jail," he told the crowd. "They can jail us, but they can never jail the Cause."

UFWOC's battle with the Teamsters and their grower allies was far from over, but a series of legal decisions in 1971 favored the farmworkers union. Four months after Cesar's release, the California Supreme Court decided that a prior ruling against UFWOC was unconstitutional and that the union had the right to boycott Bud Antle. Later, members of the Teamsters were convicted on firearms charges and other crimes, a sure sign that they couldn't always rely on the courts to side with them.

Unwelcome Legislation

Even with the Teamsters temporarily out of the picture, Cesar still struggled to negotiate a satisfactory employment contract with the lettuce growers. Moreover, by 1972 the state governments of California and Arizona had begun discussing farm-supported legislation that threatened to prohibit boycotts and harvest-time strikes, the very tactics that Cesar relied on to win fair conditions for workers. This was yet another challenge that put Cesar and the union up against the wall. They were ready, however. In February 1972, UFWOC's parent organization, the AFL-CIO, granted to the union an independent charter. This meant that the newly renamed United Farm Workers had become a full-fledged union. From the UFW's new headquarters in La Paz—a building in Keene, California, 50 miles south of Delano—Cesar gathered resources to pursue a new strategy for the challenges ahead.

In May 1972, Arizona governor Jack Williams signed into law a Farm Bureau–sponsored bill that infringed on farmworkers' rights to strike, boycott, or even organize. Cesar responded in protest with another fast. He refused food for 24 days, a sacrifice that inspired a UFW-led drive to remove Governor Williams from office and register Mexican-American voters throughout

Cesar answers a reporter's question at a March 1, 1972, news conference. The previous month, the AFL-CIO had granted the United Farm Workers union an independent charter.

the state. A new UFW slogan—*Sí Se Puede*! ("Yes, it can be done!")—accompanied the campaign. Despite collecting 168,000 petition signatures, the UFW couldn't force a recall vote to replace the governor. However, as a result of the successful voter registration campaign, the state's leadership changed dramatically. For the first time, a number of Chicanos were elected to the Arizona state senate, state house of representatives, and local government positions.

It became increasingly clear to Cesar and the UFW that such political gains were what the farmworkers needed in California. Without political power, they were simply no match for the Teamsters and the growers, who again conspired to sign more secret contracts in 1973, leaving a large force of grape workers without proper repre-

READ MORE

To learn more about the Teamsters Union, turn to page 52.

sentation. Cesar responded by urging workers and their supporters once again to boycott grapes and to picket.

A Change in Approach

However, the goon violence continued. Even priests were attacked on the picket line, and during the summer two UFW members were murdered. Cesar made the difficult decision to call off the strike. Members simply didn't have the physical protection they needed, and until they did, he believed the UFW ought to focus on the other strategies at its disposal.

Between 1973 and 1975, the UFW continued to appeal to the general public for support against the growers. During those years, 17 million Americans boycotted table grapes and the wine companies that used non-union grapes in their products.

In September 1974, Cesar had the honor of meeting Pope Paul VI in Rome and securing his endorsement for the farm-worker cause. This helped win more support from U.S. Catholics and other groups influenced by the Vatican's official position.

In February 1975, another march attracted more attention to La Causa. In a campaign that recalled the great 1966 march to Sacramento, Cesar led marchers 110 miles from San Francisco to Modesto to protest at the headquarters of the E & J Gallo Winery. The march was a public appeal for the state to establish a labor board to protect farmworkers' rights. A total of 15,000 people gathered at Modesto on the final day of the march—a number far greater than had turned out for the original march in 1966.

The February march finally convinced California governor Jerry Brown of the need for the labor board. Brown, who showed interest in meeting some of the UFW's demands, had approached Cesar two days into the march to negotiate. As a result, the California Labor Relations Act was passed that year, establishing the labor board that Cesar and the UFW had long awaited. Cesar and the UFW could not rest easy, however. They had learned by now that they would have to hold state leaders to account.

CHAPTER FIVE

ANOTHER HUNDRED YEARS

"We have thirty years of struggle behind us," Cesar said following another successful UFW strike in 1979, "but I am spirited and encouraged. I feel I can fight another hundred years."

Throughout the 1980s and into his last days, Cesar maintained the drive that distinguished him as a tireless leader. He seemed to have an infinite reserve of energy for La Causa.

In the summer of 1988, Cesar suffered through yet another fast. This was his third major fast and his longest yet, spanning 36 days. Cesar wanted to refocus the movement and draw attention to the harmful effects of pesticides on farmworkers and the environment. Four years earlier, in 1984, the UFW had announced another grape boycott—this time to raise awareness of the dangers of pesticide use. By 1988, the issue had taken on increased urgency as reports of cancer outbreaks and birth defects among farmworkers came to light. (The boycott would continue until 2000, making it the UFW's longest boycott ever.)

To Cesar's great disappointment, the growers never heeded his demands concerning pesticides. His doctors, however, warned him that he risked death if he continued with the fast. Cesar acquiesced, and in keeping with tradition, he ended the

By August 1, 1988, two weeks into his 36-day fast to draw attention to the harmful effects of pesticides, Cesar is already visibly weakened. He is flanked by his wife, Helen, and his mother. Civil rights leader Jesse Jackson is at right.

fast with a religious ceremony on August 21, 1988, at the UFW's Forty Acres ranch. Cesar's wife and his 96-year-old mother were at his side.

Several famous people showed their support that day as well. They included Robert F. Kennedy's widow, Ethel; actors Martin Sheen and Edward James Olmos; and Jesse Jackson, a minister and civil rights leader. Jackson had the honor of being the first person to whom Cesar passed the fast, a way of continuing the public witness of the pesticide issue. Following Jackson's lead, each individual in a long chain of celebrities and leaders observed a three-day fast.

More Challenges

Two decades after Cesar held his first major fast, support for La Causa was strong. It had to be. In the years since the creation of

California's Agricultural Labor Relations Board (ALRB), the government agency had failed to follow its mandate to serve the workers' best interests. Legislation had weakened the board's power, basic funding was missing, and the 1982 election of George Deukmejian as California's governor signaled a shift toward upholding grower interests. Cesar had overseen a long campaign to file hundreds of complaints with the ALRB on behalf of workers, but many of these complaints went unanswered.

An unresponsive state government wasn't Cesar's only dilemma in the 1980s. The union was also plagued by dissension. At the end of the 1970s, the UFW had boasted 100,000 members. But as the 1980s came to a close, membership had slipped below 30,000. Some critics believed that Cesar's leadership style

"In Texas . . . It Can Be Done." Also in Arizona, Florida, and elsewhere. Though known largely for their work in California, Cesar Chavez and the UFW fought for the rights of agricultural workers across the country.

was at least partly to blame for the decline. These critics accused him of acting in an autocratic manner, alienating senior leaders.

Another criticism leveled against Cesar was that he deprived the union of experienced leadership by favoring volunteer organizers over paid employees. On this issue, however, Cesar would not be swayed. He believed that the union would do better to rely on individuals motivated by a genuine desire to help workers, rather than on organizers who might simply be looking for a paycheck. Cesar was able to point to the recent successes of the 1979 lettuce strike in the Imperial Valley as proof that the UFW could still depend on its volunteer forces. He believed that the volunteers, as before, had played an important role in winning concessions from growers, which included wage increases, a guarantee of paid union representatives, and an improved medical plan.

One Last Pilgrimage

Cesar was perpetually committed to the union and its management, and for that his body paid the price, particularly in the years following his fast in 1988. During that period he often reported to close friends that he felt exhausted. His voice rarely rose above a hushed tone.

While preparing for an appeal in a court case against a vegetable grower in April 1993, Cesar put his body on the line once again with an eight-day fast. During the trial he was visiting a friend's house near his old haunts in Yuma, Arizona. He went to bed on the night of April 22 but did not wake up the following morning. He was 66 years old. When some close friends received the sad news, they refused to believe it. They assumed he would keep going forever.

The funeral for Cesar Chavez was held on April 29. Cesar's brother Richard offered a hand with the preparations, just as he

Forty thousand mourners turned out for the funeral procession of the UFW's beloved leader on April 29, 1993. Following Cesar's wishes, he was buried in a plain pine coffin. It was made by his brother Richard.

had done in past union campaigns. Carrying out an old request of Cesar's, Richard built his brother's casket out of smooth, unvarnished pine. Plans were made for a simple burial site near the entrance of La Paz.

One of Cesar's talents was being able to assemble a large crowd, and in his death he succeeded once again. About 40,000 people paid their respects by walking in a procession that followed his casket for three miles. In the spirit of UFW's famous pilgrimages, the mourners carried union flags and banners as well as 10,000 white flowers. Joining the pilgrimage were luminaries who had supported or worked side by side with Cesar through the years, including Jesse Jackson, Ethel Kennedy, and former California governor Jerry Brown. Condolence letters were sent by Pope John Paul II as well as President Bill Clinton.

The memorial program printed a quote by Cesar that expressed his readiness to sacrifice himself for others' welfare: "I am convinced that the truest act of courage, the strongest act of manliness, is to sacrifice ourselves for others in a totally nonviolent struggle for justice. . . . To be a man is to suffer for others."

"When we are really honest with ourselves," Cesar Chavez once said, "we must admit that our lives are all that really belong to us. So, it is how we use our lives that determine what kind of [people] we are."

Few leaders in U.S. history have suffered as much or been as steadfast in realizing their mission as was Cesar Chavez. After enduring the hardships of extreme poverty, he continued to fight so that future generations of workers wouldn't suffer the way he had. Today, countless farmworkers and other migrant laborers enjoy the fruits of his vision of nonviolent

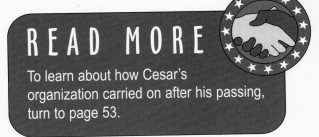

READ MORE

To learn about how Cesar's organization carried on after his passing, turn to page 53.

action, his inspiring crusades, and his noble sacrifice for La Causa. To the cynics who say, "It can't be done," those who live out Cesar's legacy say, "Sí Se Puede!"

The Tradition of Nonviolence

Many labor leaders and historians have studied the specific tactics that Cesar Chavez used in the farmworkers movement. There has been an even greater focus on the tactics of Dr. Martin Luther King Jr., a leader in the civil rights movement between 1955 and 1968. Like Cesar Chavez, King helped secure people's civil rights through a variety of nonviolent methods. These included boycotts (to a large degree, the civil rights movement took off after a 1955–1956 boycott of buses in Montgomery, Alabama), marches, and other peaceful demonstrations.

King, like Chavez, championed a type of social action known as civil disobedience. In this form of nonviolent resistance, people (often in large groups) deliberately and publicly break a law or defy a government command they consider wrong—and they willingly accept the punishment. The purpose is to draw attention to injustices, to prick the public's conscience, and ultimately to change unjust laws and government policies.

The nonviolent campaigns of the civil rights movement helped lead to major advances in the treatment of African Americans. Among the most significant gains were the Civil Rights Act of 1964 and the Voting Rights Act of 1965, as well as the dismantling of Jim Crow, the oppressive system of legally upheld racial segregation and discrimination against blacks in the South.

The views of King and Chavez toward nonviolence were greatly inspired by Mohandas Gandhi, who in turn was influenced by two writers credited as founders of nonviolent theory: the Russian novelist Leo Tolstoy (1828–1910) and the American philosopher Henry David Thoreau (1817–1862). For many advocates, Thoreau's essay *Civil Disobedience*, published in 1849, is the founding document of nonviolent philosophy.

Towering figures of nonviolent social action. Large photo: Martin Luther King Jr.
Top inset: Henry David Thoreau. Bottom inset: Leo Tolstoy.

CROSS-CURRENTS

A Kindred Spirit

Many Americans became aware of the awful conditions that existed in California's labor camps during the 1930s by reading the novels of John Steinbeck (1902–1968), a writer who closely followed the lives of America's working class. Many of his stories are set along the state's central coast, a region Cesar knew well as a farmworker and later as an organizer. The San Joaquin Valley–based DiGiorgio Corporation—one of the main targets of the 1965 grape boycott—served as a model for the Gregorios, the growers of Steinbeck's epic *The Grapes of Wrath*, published in 1939.

Although they never knew each other, Cesar and Steinbeck shared views about the labor system. To protect the rights of farmworkers, both pushed for the creation of a California agricultural labor relations board (although Steinbeck would not live to see it finally established in 1975), and both men refused to accept that the workers who toiled so hard must remain so poor. "Is it possible that this state is so stupid, so vicious, and so greedy that it cannot clothe and feed the men and women who help to make it the richest area in the world?" Steinbeck asked in an essay written in 1938. "Must the hunger become anger and anger fury before anything will be done?"

American novelist John Steinbeck wrote about the tribulations of migrant workers in his 1939 masterpiece, *The Grapes of Wrath*.

A Common Injustice

The 14th Amendment to the Constitution, ratified in 1868, guaranteed equal protection under the law to all U.S. citizens. Nevertheless, for nearly a century afterward, racial segregation endured in much of the country. While it was most systematic in the South, segregation also existed in the Southwest and California, where Cesar Chavez lived. African Americans were the principal victims of the unfair treatment bred by segregation, although hundreds of thousands of other nonwhite citizens were also forced to attend separate schools, use separate restrooms, and restrict themselves to public areas specially designated for them.

A turning point in the movement to desegregate schools and other public places was the landmark U.S. Supreme Court decision in 1954 known as *Brown v. Board of Education of Topeka*. However, it was an earlier case involving a group of Mexican-Americans that helped establish a legal precedent for *Brown v. Board*. In the 1946 case, known as *Mendez v. Westminster School District*, a California federal court ruled that segregation violated the legal rights of Mexican and Mexican-American students in Orange County.

In the years following these judicial decisions, many Americans still resisted integration efforts on the local and state levels. It took a steadfast political movement and countless acts of civil disobedience—like the one Cesar committed in a Delano movie theater—to dismantle segregation for good.

The plaintiffs in *Brown v. Board of Education*. The landmark case helped end legalized segregation in the United States.

History of the Bracero Program

Cesar hoped for fair working conditions for all laborers, including those who migrated from Mexico through the Bracero Program. Established in 1942, this program was a collaborative effort between the Mexican and American governments to bring impoverished peasants from rural Mexico to the United States as temporary guest workers. The Mexican laborers, or braceros (from the Spanish word *brazos*, meaning "arms") helped fill a major shortage of American agricultural workers brought about by the U.S. entry into World War II. But even after the war was over and American soldiers had returned home, growers in California and the Southwest continued to employ braceros because of their willingness to work for much less than U.S. laborers, and under horrible conditions that American-born workers would be unlikely to tolerate.

Responding to pressure from the agricultural industry, the U.S. government kept the Bracero Program going until 1964—by which time an estimated 4 million Mexicans had participated. The presence of large numbers of braceros created a major obstacle for Cesar Chavez and other union leaders. Simply put, the growers had no incentive to negotiate with the union when they could get the laborers they needed under the terms they set. Yet, rather than blaming the braceros, who were simply trying to make a living, Cesar sought to demonstrate how the system harmed American and Mexican farmworkers alike. It kept wages low for everyone, locked Americans out of jobs, and allowed growers to exploit powerless Mexicans.

Braceros harvest chili peppers in California, early 1960s.

A Special Kind of Suffering

Many outsiders who followed Cesar's life could not relate to his fascination with the act of fasting. Cesar was drawing inspiration from the traditions of the Mexican Catholic Church, which put a heavy emphasis on penance and suffering for the sake of a higher cause. He also was following the example of his personal hero, Mohandas Gandhi, who is reported to have fasted a total of 17 times during his life, sometimes for a month or more.

Gandhi set an example for Cesar by directing his fasts to his own people and their particular concerns. One of Gandhi's best-known fasts, in 1924, was declared in hopes of fostering more harmony between India's Hindus and Muslims, whose bitter relations threatened their chance of gaining independence from their common foe, the British colonialists. Biographer Louis Fischer writes that as Gandhi prepared to end this fast, on the 21st day, he asked his friends to "lay down their lives, if need be, for the cause of brotherhood."

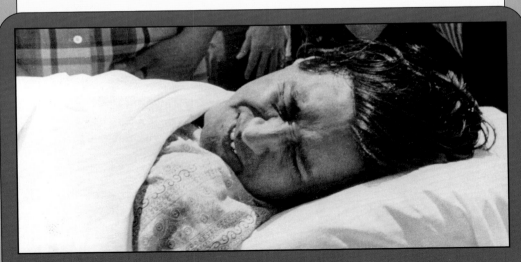

A grimace of pain on his face, Cesar Chavez lies in a hospital bed in Phoenix during his 1972 fast for the rights of Arizona farmworkers. The fast lasted 25 days.

A Powerful Union

The International Brotherhood of Teamsters was one of the most influential American labor unions during the 20th century. Originally, the word *teamster* referred to a person employed to drive a team of horses or mules, but now the word more commonly signifies a truck driver. The Teamsters Union is still active today and represents many employees in the transportation field.

When the anti-UFW contingent of Teamsters was prosecuted during the 1970s, the Teamsters suffered bad publicity. However, this was not the first time the organization had clashed with the law. One of the union's most famous leaders, Jimmy Hoffa—who as president helped the Teamsters grow to over 2 million members—was the object of a long federal investigation. In 1964, he was finally convicted of attempted bribery of a grand juror. He received a 13-year sentence, which he began serving in 1967, after his appeals had been exhausted. In late 1971, President Richard M. Nixon commuted Hoffa's sentence, and he was released from prison.

Hoffa's demise is perhaps the most intriguing part of the story. He was alleged to have extensive connections to organized crime, and the mob may have played a role in his disappearance from a restaurant parking lot on July 30, 1975. Investigators believe he was murdered, although his body has never been located.

Jimmy Hoffa, president of the International Brotherhood of Teamsters, gives a speech to union members, 1961. Hoffa, like other Teamsters officials, was implicated in criminal activity, and the union's tactics often included violence and intimidation.

Life After Cesar

Since Cesar's death in 1993, individuals and civic groups alike have paid tribute to the civil rights leader in a variety of ways. Cesar's family and friends created the Cesar E. Chavez Foundation, a nonprofit organization committed to preserving his values and vision. In August 1994, Helen Chavez was presented the Presidential Medal of Freedom, the country's highest civilian award, in Cesar's honor. Several U.S. states also recognize March 31, Cesar's birthday, as an official holiday.

Yet most would agree that the best tribute Cesar could receive is a thriving, effective farmworker union. Under the leadership of Cesar's son-in-law, Arturo Rodriguez, who became UFW president in 1993, the union has focused on winning ranch elections, signing major contracts with employers, and lobbying for worker-friendly legislation. One of the union's greatest achievements under Rodriguez was the launching of a mass campaign in 2002 that convinced Governor Gray Davis to sign a law improving the mediation process between growers and union representatives.

Arturo Rodriguez at a 2000 rally in California. A veteran UFW organizer, Rodriguez took over as president of the union after the 1993 death of Cesar Chavez, his father-in-law. Among his major priorities has been lobbying for worker-friendly legislation.

Chronology

1927: Cesar Estrada Chavez is born to Librado and Juana Chavez on March 31 outside Yuma, Arizona.

1937: Impoverished by drought conditions and hard times, the Chavez family moves to California in search of farmwork.

1948: Cesar marries Helen Fabela, and they settle in Delano, California.

1952: Cesar meets mentor Fred Ross and becomes an organizer for the Community Service Organization.

1959: He receives a promotion to CSO executive director and is transferred to Los Angeles.

1962: He resigns from the CSO and moves back to Delano to establish the National Farm Workers Association, which has its first convention on September 30.

1965: Under Cesar's leadership, the NFWA—in conjunction with a largely Filipino-American union, the Agricultural Workers Organizing Committee (AWOC)—launches the Delano grape strike campaign.

1966: NFWA and AWOC merge to form the United Farm Workers Organizing Committee (UFWOC). Cesar leads a 300-mile march from Delano to Sacramento, California's capital, to raise awareness about farmworker issues.

1968: Cesar calls for a national boycott of grapes and goes on a 25-day fast to receive a pledge of nonviolence from workers.

1970: The five-year grape boycott ends with negotiations with grape growers. A long standoff begins with the Teamsters, a rival union.

1975: Cesar calls for a new international boycott of grapes and helps negotiate the California State Legislature's enactment of the Agricultural Labor Relations Act (ALRA); in February, he leads a 110-mile protest march from San Francisco to Modesto.

1988: On August 21, he completes a 36-day "Fast for Life" to protest the growers' use of pesticides.

1993: Cesar Chavez dies in his sleep on April 23. About 40,000 people attend his funeral at UFW's headquarters.

1994: On August 8, Helen Chavez receives the Presidential Medal of Freedom in Cesar's honor.

Accomplishments/Awards

NFWA/UFWOC/UFW president, 1962–1993

Martin Luther King Nonviolent Peace Award, 1974

Nobel Peace Prize Nominee (with Helder Camara), 1971, 1974, 1975

Order of the Aztec Eagle (awarded by Mexico's foreign service), 1990

Pacem in Terris Award, 1992

Lifetime Achievement Award, Defense of Animals, 1992

Presidential Medal of Freedom (awarded posthumously), 1994

U.S. Department of Labor, Labor Hall of Fame Honoree, 1998

Congressional Gold Medal Nominee, 2004, 2005

California Hall of Fame Inductee, 2006

Further Reading

Dalton, Frederick John. *The Moral Vision of Cesar Chavez.* Maryknoll, NY: Orbis, 2003.

Ferriss, Susan, and Ricardo Sandoval. *The Fight in the Fields: Cesar Chavez and the Farmworkers Movement.* San Diego: Harcourt Brace, 1997.

Fischer, Louis. *Gandhi: His Life and Message for the World.* Thorndike, ME: Thorndike Press, 1983.

Levy, Jacques E. *Cesar Chavez: Autobiography of La Causa.* Minneapolis: University of Minnesota Press, 1975.

Rosales, Francisco Arturo. *Chicano!: The History of the Mexican American Civil Rights Movement.* Houston: Arte Publico Press, 1997.

Williams, Juan. *Eyes on the Prize. America's Civil Rights Years, 1954–1965.* New York: Viking, 1987.

Internet Resources

http://www.farmworkermovement.org

> The comprehensive Web site of the Farmworker Movement Documentation Project has oral history, sound clips, and personal essays written by movement figures.

http://www.ufw.org

> The official page of the United Farm Workers includes updates on the current efforts of the union and historical accounts of Cesar Chavez and the farmworker movement.

http://www.chavezfoundation.org

> The site of the Cesar E. Chavez Foundation highlights the nonprofit organization's service work and features educational resources about Cesar.

http://www.cesarchavezholiday.org

> This site provides updates on petition drives and legislative developments to commemorate Cesar's birthday as a national holiday.

http://www.pbs.org/itvs/fightfields/cesarchavez.html

> Companion site to the book *The Fight in the Fields* by Susan Ferriss and Ricardo Sandoval and the documentary film of the same name.

Glossary

autocratic—exercising unlimited powers of leadership; dictatorial.

barrio—a Spanish-speaking neighborhood in a city or town in the United States, usually in the Southwest.

boycott—a campaign in which people coordinate their refusal to have transactions with a person, store, or organization to express disapproval or force acceptance of certain conditions.

bracero—a Mexican agricultural laborer in the United States as a temporary guest worker under a program in existence between 1942 and 1964.

canvasser—a person who goes through an area to solicit orders or political support or to determine opinions or sentiments.

charter—a written document by an organization to create a local office or division.

Chicano—an American of Mexican descent.

homestead—a home and adjoining land occupied by a family.

injunction—a court order requiring an individual or group to do a specified act, or to refrain from doing a specified act.

integration—the bringing together of individuals of different groups (usually races).

mandate—a formal order from a body of government or other authority.

migrant worker—an agricultural laborer who moves around seasonally, usually to follow the planting and harvesting seasons of various crops.

nonviolence—abstention from violence for the purpose of securing political ends.

penance—an act of sacrifice or devotion performed to show sorrow or repentance for sin.

pesticide—a chemical agent used to kill insects or other pests.

picket line—a line of people (usually striking workers) walking or standing around a place of business, in order to discourage people from working at that business and thereby to force the business owner to negotiate a labor contract.

second-class citizen—a person having a socially, politically, or economically deprived status.

strike—a work stoppage designed to force business owners to negotiate with workers.

sweetheart deal—a contract that is unusually favorable for both parties and is usually executed at the expense of another party.

unconstitutional—failing to accord with the constitution of a state or society, and thus illegal.

Chapter Notes

Chapter 1: Another Victory

p. 8: "No union movement is worth . . ." Susan Ferriss and Ricardo Sandoval, *The Fight in the Fields: Cesar Chavez and the Farmworkers Movement* (San Diego: Harcourt Brace, 1997), 144.

p. 11: "one of the heroic figures . . ." Cited at Las Culturas.com, "Cesar Chavez Chronology." http://www.lasculturas.com/aa/bio/bioCesarChavezChron.htm

p. 11: "He talked about . . ." Ferriss and Sandoval, *Fight in the Fields*, 268.

Chapter 2: Crooked Lines

p. 14: "She would try . . ." Jacques E. Levy, *Cesar Chavez: Autobiography of La Causa* (Minneapolis: University of Minnesota Press, 1975), 19.

p. 16: "If we had stayed there . . . " Ibid., 42.

p. 21: "I have an announcement . . ." Ferriss and Sandoval, *Fight in the Fields*, 62.

Chapter 3: Viva La Causa!

p. 23: "What I didn't know . . ." Ferriss and Sandoval, *Fight in the Fields*, 63.

p. 25: *"Viva la causa! . . ."* "The Little Strike That Could," *Time* (July 4, 1969), 18.

p. 28: "I said, 'Okay, we've won' . . ." Levy, *Cesar Chavez*, 246.

p. 30: "Our struggle is not easy . . ." Ibid., 286.

Chapter 4: A Fearsome Rival

p. 31: "sweet grapes of justice." Levy, *Cesar Chavez*, 403.

p. 32: "It's tragic that these men . . ." Ferriss and Sandoval, *Fight in the Fields*, 162.

p. 33: "The only way . . ." Levy, *Cesar Chavez*, 292.

p. 35: "My spirit was never . . ." Ibid., 433.

Chapter 5: Another Hundred Years

p. 39: "We have thirty years . . ." Ferriss and Sandoval, *Fight in the Fields*, 216.

p. 43: "I am convinced . . ." Levy, *Cesar Chavez*, 268.

p. 44: "When we are really honest . . ." San Antonio Public Library, "Celebrating César Chávez." http://www.sanantonio.gov/Libary/events/ccc/quotes.asp

Cross-Currents

p. 48: "Is it possible that . . ." Ferriss and Sandoval, *Fight in the Fields*, 25.

p. 51: "lay down their lives . . ." Louis Fischer, *Gandhi: His Life and Message for the World* (New York: Mentor, 1982), 78.

Index

Numbers in **bold italics** refer to captions.

Photo Credits

Contributors

BRIAN BAUGHAN is a writer living in Philadelphia. He is the author of *Human Rights in Africa, Liberia, Arab-Israeli Relations: 1950–1979*, and biographies of Russell Simmons and LL Cool J.